simply romantic

Coffee Dates
for Couples

FAMILYLIFE
Publishing™

Little Rock, Arkansas

Coffee Dates for Couples
© 2006 by FamilyLife, a ministry of Campus Crusade for Christ
All rights reserved. Published 2006
Printed in India

11 10 09 08 07   2 3 4 5 6 7
ISBN: 978-1-57229-894-1

Authors: Janel Breitenstein, Margie Clark, and Amy L. Gordon
Editor: Amy L. Gordon
Proofreader: Rich Cairnes
Graphic Designer: Lee Smith
Photographer: Willie Allen

FamilyLife
Dennis Rainey, President
5800 Ranch Drive
Little Rock, Arkansas 72223
1-800-FL-TODAY • familylife.com

Contents

CAUTION: Hot contents! Coffee and conversation can reach a boiling point. Allow contents to cool. Sip carefully. Practice patience and understanding as you connect with each other.

Coffee Talk 101

Acidity

The sharp, lively quality characteristic of high-grown
coffee, tasted mainly at the tip of the tongue.
The brisk, snappy quality that makes coffee refreshing.

Americano

A shot or two of espresso that has been
poured into a glass filled with hot water.
Brewed coffee, only stronger.

Coffee Talk 101

Arabica

Common name for Coffea arabica, one of the
two principal commercial species of coffee.
Arabica accounts for approximately 70 percent
of world coffee production. Arabica is the bean
most used as "specialty" and "gourmet."

Aroma

The fragrance of coffee, either as roasted beans or brewed.

Coffee on the Go

Advice for Her: Start the conversation in the car on the way to the coffeehouse. Many men open up more when they don't have to make eye contact.

Hit the coffee shop in the local shopping mall
and browse the stores.

Gals, as you shop, ask him to choose clothes he thinks you would look good in. Guys, then let her make a few suggestions for your wardrobe as well.

Visit a bookstore with a coffee shop.
Get cozy in the travel section.

Husbands, ask your wife to describe her dream vacation:
location, activities, length of stay, etc. ...
Now, wives, it's your turn to listen.

Pick up a cup of "joe" on your way
to a home improvement store.

Walk the aisles and describe your dream home to each other, husbands going first this time. When you're through, skim the home improvement and plans books, noting features to add to your wish list.

9

This might seem a little strange, but try it anyway.
Fill a thermos with hot coffee and head over
to the nearest cemetery.

As you read the epitaphs, ask, "What would you want said about you at your funeral? For what character trait do you want to be known?"

Here's one for the holidays:
With your coffee, gloves, and loved one to keep
you warm, walk (or drive) through neighborhoods
festooned with Christmas lights.

Talk about which holiday you enjoy the most and the ways you like to celebrate it.

13

Pick up your favorite gourmet coffee on your
way to the park. Then, on the swings or seesaw,
ask your love these questions:

"What is your fondest childhood memory? Who was your favorite relative? And your favorite toy was ... ?"

simply romantic

Coffee Talk 101

Barista
A professional maker of coffee beverages;
employee of a coffee bar.

Blending
The act of combining two or more coffees, usually to
achieve a consistent flavor profile.

Coffee at Home

At home watching television ...

Every time you see coffee on the tube
or hear the word, you must kiss.
If you see steam, create some of your own.

At home under the stars ...

Talk about the five most important milestones you've reached together. Why are they important to you?

At home in the kitchen ...

After serving coffee just the way he or she likes it,
sit down and ask, "What do you look forward to today?"
Then really listen.

At home in the living room ...

Settle in with mugs of hot java and your wedding album. Take turns talking about your favorite memories from your special day.

25

At home during the holidays ...

Turn on the coffee pot, turn down the lights, put on some Christmas music, and enjoy the peace and quiet.

At home in bed ...

When you know you're free to sleep in the next morning, brew a pot of the leaded stuff to keep you up late. Start a long list of the things that you find sexy in your spouse. Follow up with visual aids and demonstrations!

29

Coffee Talk 101

Body

Coffee taster's perception of the weight, richness, and thickness of the flavor. Also referred to as "mouth feel."

Café au lait

A traditional French drink made with equal portions of brewed coffee and steamed milk.

Coffee Talk 101

Cappuccino

A coffee beverage made from espresso and steamed milk, capped with milk foam.

Complexity

A quality of coffee that gives multiple taste sensations.

Coffee Talk 101

Earthy

A flavor sometimes desired, more often not, caused by less-than-optimal processing, giving coffee the taste of dirt. Frequently found in Indonesian coffees.

Espresso

A concentrated coffee beverage made by forcing water under pressure through finely ground coffee. Used for making a variety of exotic coffee drinks.

Coffee off the Beaten Path

All-Night Diner

Cozy up in the kitsch of an all-night diner.
Over your bottomless cups of joe, swap stories
about the strangers who come and go, explaining
to each other what keeps them up at this late hour.

35

Upscale Restaurant

As you sip your espresso and finish dessert, decide
to which charity you would give $100,000—assuming
that you had the money to give. If that act of
generosity is out of your budget, find one that isn't.

Outdoor High School Sporting Event

Ask each other, "To what were you most committed in high school—music, schoolwork, sports, boyfriend/girlfriend, friends, car, work, family, or a club/group?"

39

Out-of-Town Coffee Shop

Discuss where on earth you would most like to meet for coffee. Choose a city or region on each continent.

Your In-Laws' House

Arrange to have coffee with your in-laws.
While sipping your coffee, play footsie with your spouse.
Don't laugh—at least while you're at the table.

Homeless Shelter

Volunteer to serve coffee at a nearby homeless shelter.
Take time to talk to a resident and learn part
of his or her life story.

45

Coffee Talk 101

Frappuccino
A coffee slush, blending iced coffee,
milk, flavorings, and ice.

French Roast
A coffee (not necessarily from France) that has been
roasted so as to bring out the oils in the beans.
This process gives the finished product
a somewhat bittersweet flavor.

Coffeehouse
Conversations

Cozy up in the corner of your favorite coffeehouse and connect over each of these conversation starters.

If a movie were made about your life,
whom would you like to play the lead role? Why?

If you could have any super power,
what would it be? Why?

Create a fun date on a $10 budget.
Note your ideas on a napkin and plan for later.

51

How do you imagine God?
In your mind, what does heaven look like?

Of all the items that have been or are in production today, which would you like to have invented? Why?

If you were forced to give up one of your five senses,
which would you choose to lose—
sight, hearing, touch, taste, or smell?

If you were a car, what type of car would you be and why? In life, which gear are you in— reverse, neutral, drive, or overdrive?

Tell your spouse what he or she did that won your heart.
Explain why it worked.

Gals, order the beverage most like your hubby.
Is he hot, strong, and straightforward?
Then drink black coffee.
As you make your comparisons,
be sure he (and no one else) notices
how you lick the edge of your cup.

FACT: Coffee has been scientifically linked to improving sexual functions in men and women.

Coffee Talk 101

Froth
Thick, foamy milk. The result of steam aeration.

Fruity
A flavor that reminds the taster of fruit,
this quality is generally considered an asset.

Coffee Talk 101

Italian Roast

Definition varies by region. Considered the darkest
roast to people on the East Coast of the U.S.,
as compared to French roast, which is considered
darkest to those on the West Coast.

Latte

A beverage created by mixing espresso and steamed milk.
May or may not be topped off with milk foam.

Coffee Around
the World

ITALY

Coffea

Find a quaint little Italian restaurant
and enjoy a *coffea* and dessert.
Discuss: Which Italian city would you most like to visit—
Rome, Florence, Milan, Naples, or Venice? Why?

HAWAII

Kope

While enjoying a cup of *kope*, plan a dream
vacation to Hawaii. Now figure out how
you can make your dream a reality.

GREECE

Kafes

In Greece, the eldest is customarily served *kafes* first.
Take turns naming and describing adults from
your youth who had an impact on your life.

JAPAN

Koohii

The Japanese are known to bathe in coffee grounds fermented with pineapple pulp. Consider sipping *koohii* together in a coffee-scented bubble bath.

FRANCE

Café

On July 12, 1789, Camille Desmoulins called his fellow citizens to arms while standing on a table in the Café de Foy coffeehouse. Two days later the French Revolution began. If you could change one thing in the world today, what would it be?

ETHIOPIA

Buni

Ethiopia is the birthplace of coffee.
In five minutes or less, tell your spouse everything
you remember about your birthplace.

Coffee Talk 101

Macchiato
Italian for "marked." Foamed milk on top of an ounce-and-a-half of espresso. Served in a demitasse.

Mellow
Having well-rounded flavor that results when sugar combines with the salts in coffee, causing a slightly sweet sensation. Hawaiian Kona coffee is considered mellow.

Coffee Questions
and Quizzes

Wives, how would you describe your husband's
personality using these coffee terms?

hot	fresh
robust	soft
sweet	strong
spicy	creamy
delicate	mild
smooth	unique
nutty	balanced
mellow	wild

Husbands, how would you describe your wife's
personality using these coffee terms?

hot	fresh
robust	soft
sweet	strong
spicy	creamy
delicate	mild
smooth	unique
nutty	balanced
mellow	wild

Of the following accessories to your coffee ritual,
which is non-negotiable?

❏ travel mug
❏ coffeemaker with timer
❏ cash for coffeehouse visits
❏ cup holder in my car
❏ creamer/sugar
❏ other

Of the following accessories to your relationship,
which is most important to you?

- ❏ hugs
- ❏ kisses
- ❏ cuddling
- ❏ making love
- ❏ listening
- ❏ encouragement
- ❏ gifts
- ❏ acts of kindness
- ❏ quality time together

If you could travel through time, which of these historical coffeehouse events would you attend? Why?

1732

The debut performance of Johann Sebastian Bach's famous *Coffee Cantata* is given at a coffeehouse in Germany.

1761

One hundred fifty stockbrokers meet at Jonathan's Coffee-House to form a club which will later become the London Stock Exchange.

1776

The Declaration of Independence is read to the public for the first time at the Merchant's Coffee House in Philadelphia, Pennsylvania.

81

Here is a famous coffee slogan: "The best part of wakin' up is Folgers in your cup." What is the best part of waking up for you and your spouse?

Finish this acrostic of your sweetie's best character qualities:

My wife is ...

C_____
O_____
F_____
F_____
E_____
E_____

My husband is ...

C_____
O_____
F_____
F_____
E_____
E_____

Which coffee blend best describes you as a lover?

Jamaican Blue Mountain: full-bodied and smooth
Peaberry's Special: bright, bold, juicy, and rare
Mocha Java: complex and full-bodied

84

Which coffee blend best describes you as a lover?

Breakfast Blend: bright, light-bodied, and mild
Italian Roast: intense, full-bodied, robust, and spicy
Costa Rica Reserve: deep, pungent, with a hint of smokiness

Coffee Talk 101

Mocha

A latte with chocolate syrup added. May be topped with whipped cream and cocoa powder or shaved chocolate.

Nutty

Having a flavor that reminds the coffee taster of almonds or other nuts.

Coffee Talk 101

Robusta

About 30 percent of the coffee grown in the world is robusta. The scientific name is *Coffea canephora*. Usually less acidic and aromatic than Arabica, sometimes bitter.

Solo

A single shot of espresso.

Coffee Talk 101

Tone
The color of brewed coffee (e.g., light- or dark-toned).

Woody
Having an unpleasant wood-like taste.

Coffee Warm-Ups

Coffee has two virtues. It is wet and it is warm.
—Old Dutch saying

Brew some steamy, stimulating conversation
with these more *intimate* questions ...

Which physical characteristic do you most admire in your spouse? Why? Be sure to give it special attention before turning out the lights.

As a couple, what do you wish you had more time for?
Talk about ways to carve time in your schedule.

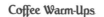

How can you show more love and respect to your spouse?

Talk about your sex life. Share what you enjoy, ask how you can improve it, and find out what your spouse wishes you would or wouldn't do.

Would it be harder for you to give up chocolate, coffee, or sex? Answer honestly! Of the three, which two are the best together? Try a sample. (HINT: extra point for bringing chocolate-covered coffee beans to the bedroom!)

simply romantic

95

Think back to your first cup of coffee together.
Where were you and what brought you together?

What is that certain something your spouse does that really turns you on? Tonight, experiment and add another "something" to each other's list.

What board game or video game
best describes your love life?

How can you turn your coffee dates into foreplay?

simply romantic

99

When is the ideal time for sex? Life too crazy?
Take a few minutes to plan some "quickies."

Who usually takes the initiative in the bedroom?
Figure out how to reverse the roles once in a while.

101

Coffee Memories

Best cup of coffee ever _____

Worst cup of coffee ever _____

Strangest place you've ever had coffee _____

Favorite coffee shop _____

Coffee Memories

Most romantic place to drink coffee _____

Best mood music for good coffee _____

Best time of day for coffee _____

Best coffee-drinking activity _____

Café Borgia
makes 4 servings

2 cups strong Italian coffee
2 cups hot chocolate
whipped cream
grated orange peel

1. Mix coffee and hot chocolate.
2. Pour into mugs.
3. Top with whipped cream and orange peel.

Turkish Coffee
makes 4 servings

1 1/2 cups cold water
4 teaspoons dark roast coffee (ground very fine)
4 teaspoons sugar

1. Heat water in saucepan, add coffee and sugar when warm.
2. Bring to boil.
3. Pour half of the coffee into demitasse cups.
4. Return remaining coffee to stove, and allow to return to boil.
5. Spoon off foam, and gently place into each cup (don't stir).

simply romantic

105

Fan the flames of romance!

Tips to Romance Your Husband and *Tips to Romance Your Wife* bring spark and sizzle to your marriage. Learn to communicate heart-to-heart, express love through food and fun, give gifts that say, "I love you!" and romance your love on birthdays and holidays. Heat up your marriage with these creative ideas and become *Simply Romantic!*

Acknowledgments

Thanks to Roger Cheuvront of Java Roasting Company in Little Rock, Arkansas, for providing a wonderful atmosphere for content inspiration and the photo shoot.

Our appreciation is also extended to Willie Allen, photographer extraordinaire, and Lee Smith, creative director and designer on this project.

We'd also like to acknowledge Gregg Stutts, Jerry McCall, and Stephanie Bryant for their coffee date ideas.